SPORTS HEROES AND LEGENDS

Peyton Manning

Read all of the books in this exciting, action-packed biography series!

Hank Aaron

Muhammad Ali

Lance Armstrong

David Beckham

Barry Bonds

Roberto Clemente

Sasha Cohen

Joe DiMaggio

Tim Duncan

Dale Earnhardt Jr.

Doug Flutie

Lou Gehrig

Wayne Gretzky

Mia Hamm

Tony Hawk

Derek Jeter

Michael Jordan

Sandy Koufax

Michelle Kwan

Eli Manning

Peyton Manning

Mickey Mantle

Shaquille O'Neal

Jesse Owens

Cal Ripken Jr.

Jackie Robinson

Alex Rodriguez

Wilma Rudolph

Babe Ruth

Annika Sorenstam

Ichiro Suzuki

Jim Thorpe

Tiger Woods

SPORTS HEROES AND LEGENDS

Peyton Manning

by Matt Doeden

BARNES & NOBLE

NEW YORK

Contents

Big-Game Quarterback

"Peyton Manning can't win the big game." Twenty-seven-year-old Peyton Manning had heard that comment time and again for several years. The Indianapolis Colts quarterback had lost each of his first three National Football League (NFL) playoff games. He was one of the league's best quarterbacks during the regular season, but for some reason, he just hadn't been able to get it done in the playoffs.

So on January 4, 2004, when Peyton stepped onto the field of the RCA Dome in Indianapolis, Indiana, for a first-round playoff game against the Denver Broncos, he knew that the pressure was on. All eyes would be on him. Would he finally prove that he was indeed a big-game quarterback? Or would yet another playoff loss make the criticism even louder?

Peyton and the Colts knew there was one way to answer the critics. On their first drive of the game, they marched down the field against the Broncos' defense. Peyton completed all four passes he attempted on the drive, capping it off with a 31-yard touchdown to receiver Brandon Stokley. The Broncos answered with a field goal of their own, but the Colts didn't let up on their second possession. One of the game's most memorable plays came from the Colts at the Broncos' 46-yard line. Peyton rifled a pass to receiver Marvin Harrison. Harrison caught the ball and fell to the turf. Several Bronco defenders surrounded him, but none of them actually touched him to end the play. So Harrison rolled over, got up, and darted 30 yards into the end zone for a 14–3 Indianapolis lead.

It was just one play, but it summed up the game. Peyton was playing flawlessly. He stood calmly behind his offensive line, finding receivers downfield and hitting them with one laser-sharp pass after the next. He found Harrison for another touchdown. Then he connected with Reggie Wayne to set up a field goal. Denver was unable to stop the onslaught.

"That was a great game plan and it was executed as well as I've ever seen," said Denver coach Mike Shanahan. "We came into a hornet's nest. Once [Peyton] gets a beat on you, he is hard to stop."

The domination continued in the second half. The Colts scored every time they got the ball until early in the fourth quarter. By that time, the game was a blowout. Peyton was watching from the sidelines. He'd had a nearly perfect game, completing 22 of 26 passes for 377 yards and a jaw-dropping 5 touchdowns. By the final whistle, Peyton and his teammates were celebrating one of the most lopsided wins in NFL playoff history, 41–10.

"I hope people think this was a big game," said Colts head coach Tony Dungy after the game. "We kept hearing about Peyton's failure to win big games. I guess this was a big one."

Chapter | One

Born a Manning

For NFL fans old and young alike, the name *Manning* conjures an image of a calm, cool quarterback dropping back behind his line and hitting receivers with crisp, accurate passes. It's a family tradition that little Peyton Williams Manning was born into on March 24, 1976, in New Orleans, Louisiana.

Peyton, the second son of Olivia and Archie Manning, seemed destined to be a football player. Archie was already a five-year veteran of the NFL when Peyton was born. After turning himself into a college football legend at Ole Miss (the University of Mississippi), Archie was the second overall pick of the 1971 NFL Draft. The elder Manning was an instant star for his new team, the New Orleans Saints. He wowed fans with his poise in the pocket, his pinpoint accuracy, and his elusive scrambling. Unfortunately, the Saints were one of the NFL's worst teams at that time. Even a young, electrifying quarterback couldn't lift them to so much as a winning season during Archie's years with the team.

In 1978, Archie was named Player of the Year in the National Football Conference (NFC). He passed for 3,416 yards and 17 touchdowns.

But soon, football became the second most important thing in Archie Manning's life. Nothing came before family. His three sons—Cooper, Peyton, and Eli—always came first.

"There are a lot of days when [Dad] got beat up on the field and [the Saints] lost badly," Peyton later said. "He never brought his sorrows home. . . . When he came home . . . you'd [have] thought he had just won the Super Bowl."

It's no surprise that football was a big source of bonding between father and sons. For Cooper, Peyton, and Eli, playing and watching the game was a way of life. Inside or outside—or on the field of the Louisiana Superdome—they were always emulating their famous father. Peyton may have been the biggest football fan of the three. He had some old audiotapes of his dad's games at Ole Miss. He'd sit and listen to them over and over. He loved hearing his dad's name called.

Despite Archie's efforts to spend time with his family, the life of an NFL player is demanding. When Archie finally left the Saints to play for the Houston Oilers (1982–1983) and then the Minnesota Vikings (1983–1984), Olivia and the boys stayed behind in New Orleans. It was hard on the family. Archie sometimes would fly home right after practice, eat supper with Olivia and the boys, then get on another plane and get back to work.

RELIVING THE GLORY

Peyton loved to listen to audiotapes of Archie's college football games at Ole Miss. He would spend hours in his room reliving games that had happened more than a decade earlier. "[Dad] was my favorite player growing up," Peyton later said. "That's why I wanted to know everything about him, in his college era and his pro era. . . . It's neat to have your hero in your own living room."

The 1984 season was Archie's last. He couldn't stand being away any longer, so he retired from football and took a job announcing Saints games on the radio. From that point, Cooper, Peyton, and Eli had their dad around all the time.

"When I finally left the Vikings, it was an upper instead of a downer," Archie later wrote. "Good-bye, football, hello, rest of my life. And hello, Cooper, Peyton, and Eli, and the football I would enjoy through them. A whole new world."

All three boys inherited Archie's athletic talent and love of sports. They competed fiercely with one another—especially Cooper and Peyton, who were separated by just two years. (Eli was five years younger than Peyton, but he did his best to keep up.) Arguments and fights between the boys were part of daily life at the Manning home.

Peyton and his brothers attended the Isidore Newman private school in New Orleans. To no one's surprise, Peyton went out for the football team when he entered seventh grade. His junior high coaches quickly realized that Peyton was special. He wasn't like any seventh-grade quarterback they'd ever seen. He had all the tools—a great arm, natural athleticism, and a remarkable understanding of the game.

Football wasn't the only sport Peyton liked to play. He also spent time on Newman's basketball and baseball teams. For a while, he even hoped to play baseball as well as football in college.

Normally, a junior high team doesn't do much passing. But with Peyton, the pass was a big part of Newman's offense. And it wasn't just simple, straightforward passing. Peyton was throwing deep bombs and complicated crossing routes, in which a receiver cuts across the middle of the field and the heart of the defense.

As Archie and Cooper watched one of Peyton's first games, Archie commented on how well Peyton was doing. "What the heck did you expect?" asked Peyton's older brother. "He's been doing it all his life."

By tenth grade, Peyton was really turning heads. It was the fall of 1991, and Peyton took over as Newman's varsity quarterback. His favorite receiver was Cooper, who was in twelfth grade. It was an amazing season for Peyton and the Mannings. Even today, he says it's the most fun he's ever had playing football. The Manning-to-Manning connection was big news. The boys even appeared with their dad on the cover of a local high school football magazine.

Peyton was a star athlete, but he was also an excellent student. He was named to the Blue Chip Academic All-America Team in 1993.

The team lived up to the hype. Newman went 9–1 in the regular season, then advanced to the semifinals of the

Louisiana State playoffs. By this time, college scouts were getting a close look at both Manning boys. Because Cooper was a senior, he got most of the attention. But the scouts also kept a close eye on the team's star sophomore quarterback.

Cooper wanted to follow in Archie's footsteps. He accepted a scholarship to play wide receiver at Ole Miss. But before his college football career ever got off the ground, it came to a quick and scary end. Doctors diagnosed him with spinal stenosis, a narrowing of the spinal column in the neck. Cooper would never play competitive football again.

❝ *It was a treat coaching [Peyton]. It's something every coach hopes comes around one time in his coaching career. You're not only dealing with a fine athlete but a really great person with extraordinary character and leadership abilities. He had it all.*❞

—Frank Gendusa, one of Peyton's
high school football coaches

Peyton, however, did not share his brother's condition, and he continued to excel as Newman's quarterback. His 30 touchdown passes in 1992 led the team to the state quarterfinals. He did even better in 1993, his final high school season. He threw 39 touchdown passes and led Newman to an undefeated regular season. But the team lost in the second round of the playoffs. Peyton's dreams of a high school state title weren't to be. Still, he had plenty to look forward to. It was time to continue his career in college. But where?

Chapter | Two

The Volunteer

O le Miss fans and college football fans across the nation assumed that Peyton would carry on the family tradition in Mississippi. But with Cooper's football career over, Peyton wasn't so sure. He'd always imagined playing college football with his brother, but that couldn't happen anymore. Was Ole Miss still the right choice? The school's football program was struggling. Peyton felt that he owed it to himself to at least look at some other schools. Coaches from college football power-houses like Michigan, Notre Dame, and Tennessee came calling.

Archie was quietly hoping his second son would go to Ole Miss. But Peyton had a good feeling about the Tennessee Volunteers (nicknamed the Vols). "For some reason, Tennessee felt right," he later wrote.

Still, Peyton remained deliberate. It was a big decision, and he carefully weighed all of his options. Which school had the

11

best program? Which coach did he like best? Where would he get a chance to play right away?

During the college football recruiting season, Peyton got as many as 30 calls a day from interested coaches.

The answer kept coming back the same: Tennessee. His mind was made up, and Archie happily supported his son's decision, even though he knew that Ole Miss fans would be disappointed. Peyton and Archie quickly called a press conference and announced that Peyton would attend the University of Tennessee.

The reaction they got from Ole Miss fans was shocking. Calls and letters blasted both Peyton and Archie. Many fans were furious at Archie for not forcing his son to attend Ole Miss. Many of the letters were just plain mean. "I hope you get hurt," wrote one Ole Miss supporter. Another claimed, "We always loved your dad, but not after this."

Despite it all, Peyton felt good about his decision. Tennessee was a team on the rise. It had a base of rabidly loyal fans, and every one of them was excited about Peyton. Eager to get a start on his academic career, Peyton enrolled in summer classes in July

1994, shortly after his high school graduation. Football practice soon followed, and Peyton was ready to go. He'd show up an hour before practice started. He'd stay late. His friends nicknamed him "Caveman" because he spent so much time studying past games in the team's dark film room. He later described himself as "determined to the point of being obsessed."

Peyton knew that he needed to work hard because of the heavy competition at the quarterback spot. Senior Jerry Colquitt was in line to take the starting role. Junior Todd Helton (who later became a star first baseman for baseball's Colorado Rockies) also brought experience to the position. And fellow freshman recruit Branndon Stewart was also in the mix. But while all were athletically gifted, none had Peyton's fanatical attention to detail. More than anyone else, Peyton lived and breathed football. Stewart was a better pure athlete than Peyton, but Peyton was the smarter, more informed quarterback.

❝During the fall, I asked so many questions, Coach Cutcliffe told me I'd give him an ulcer. . . . My number one priority was to be a student of the game.❞

—PEYTON ON HIS FRESHMAN YEAR AT TENNESSEE

Peyton didn't expect to see any action in the team's season opener against the University of California, Los Angeles (UCLA).

But Colquitt got hurt in the first quarter. Helton came in but was ineffective. Tennessee was losing 18–0, and the offense was stagnant. Finally, the coaches told Peyton to warm up. He was going in! Peyton played just three plays. He didn't impress anyone. Stewart played the next series and was also ineffective. Helton finished the game—a 25–23 UCLA victory.

Peyton played little during the next two games. But in the team's fourth game, versus Mississippi State, Helton got hurt. Tennessee's coaching staff had to choose between Peyton and Stewart. They decided that Peyton was more mentally prepared to take over. This time, Peyton was ready. On his third play, he took the snap and dropped back to pass. He surveyed the field and saw receiver Kendrick Jones streaking down the sideline. Peyton stepped up and fired a deep pass. His accuracy was spot-on. Jones caught the ball in stride and dashed all the way to the end zone for a 76-yard touchdown!

For a moment, Peyton just stood there, staring. He'd done it! It was his first touchdown pass as a Volunteer. He played most of the rest of the game, going 14 of 23 (14 completions in 23 pass attempts) for 256 yards and 2 touchdowns. Stewart also saw some playing time, but he struggled. He threw an untimely interception that put a damper on the Vols' momentum. That interception was a big reason Tennessee lost the game, 24–21.

Peyton's good day earned him the starting quarterback spot against Washington State, which had one of the best defenses in college football. Tennessee won the game 10–9, but Peyton didn't play well, completing just 7 passes. He struggled again the next week against Alabama. His talent was evident, but he was playing like an inexperienced freshman. He'd look brilliant on one play and clueless on the next.

A quarterback controversy between Peyton and Stewart was heating up. The truth was that both freshmen were still making rookie mistakes. But Stewart's parents were furious at what they saw as special treatment given to Peyton. They thought that the coaches were favoring Peyton because of his famous father and went so far as to cheer when Peyton made bad plays. They even drove up to Tennessee to talk to the coaches. They felt that their son wasn't getting a fair shot.

"Truth be known, Peyton was much more prepared to play," said Tennessee offensive coordinator David Cutcliffe. "Peyton outworked Branndon."

Peyton got the start again against Kentucky. He needed to perform. The impatient Tennessee fans had started to boo their young quarterback. But Peyton quickly silenced his critics. He led the Vols to a 52–0 blowout, then followed that with a 65–0 thrashing of Vanderbilt. The Vols were on a roll and earned a trip to the Gator Bowl, where they faced powerful Virginia Tech.

The Vols capitalized on their momentum and rolled to yet another victory, 45–23. The highlight of the game for Peyton was a rare 29-yard run. He'd been labeled as a slow, immobile quarterback who couldn't do much damage with his legs. Proudly, he announced, "I can run, too."

THE WOMAN IN PEYTON'S LIFE

Peyton was focused on football and his classes at Tennessee. But he also made time for a social life. He even had a steady girlfriend, Ashley Thompson. The couple had been introduced by Ashley's neighbor. Ashley was going to school at the University of Virginia, but the two tried to get together as often as they could.

For his roller-coaster season, Peyton was named Southeastern Conference (SEC) Freshman of the Year. He threw 11 touchdown passes and just 6 interceptions in about half a season's worth of snaps. The writing was on the wall: This was Peyton's team. Stewart transferred to Texas A&M, where he could get more playing time.

Peyton was excited to get his sophomore season started in the fall of 1995. But although he had secured his status as the team's starting quarterback, he wasn't satisfied. He'd discovered a flaw in his throwing motion. "My first year, I found myself bringing the ball lower," he said. "The motion was good. It was just taking longer to get rid of the ball."

During the off-season, he worked on a new grip that would speed up his release time. The change paid immediate dividends. The Vols beat East Carolina in the 1995 opener. But the true test came against powerful Georgia in the second game, aired nationally on the ESPN television network. Peyton didn't disappoint, going 26 of 38 for 349 yards and 2 touchdowns. To top it off, he led a last-minute drive for the winning field goal.

All the good feelings came crashing down in the next game, versus Florida. The Gators destroyed Tennessee, 62–37. It was a humbling, embarrassing loss for the whole team. But it was also the only game the Vols would lose during the regular season. Peyton and his teammates quickly bounced back with an eight-game winning streak. Peyton was razor sharp. His rare combination of arm strength, accuracy, and almost flawless decision making made him a handful for any defense. He and star receiver Joey Kent were connecting for touchdown after touchdown.

Opposing defenses seemed almost helpless. Against Arkansas, Peyton went 35 of 46 for 384 yards and 4 touchdowns. Against archrival Alabama, he and Kent hooked up for a thrilling 80-yard touchdown pass and a 41–14 victory.

Life was good for Tennessee fans. By the end of the regular season, the Vols were 10–1 and ranked fourth in the nation (tied with Ohio State). Peyton was exceeding all expectations.

Left Out

After Tennessee's 41–14 win over Alabama—one of the biggest wins of Peyton's young college career—Peyton found himself talking to a television reporter while his teammates were celebrating in the end zone. With a scowl, Peyton let the reporter know that he didn't appreciate being left out of the celebration. Many players would have jumped at a chance for a national television interview, but Peyton just wanted to be with his teammates. "Everybody over there was going crazy and I didn't get to get [in on] any of it," he said. "It bothered me."

As the SEC's second-best team, Tennessee was rewarded with an invitation to the Citrus Bowl, where they would face off with the powerful Ohio State Buckeyes. The Vols weren't intimidated, though. They won a hard-fought, rain-soaked, defensive battle, 20–14. Peyton went 20 of 35 for 182 yards and a touchdown pass. Better yet, he was 2–0 in bowl games in his short career.

Peyton had had quite a season. He had thrown for 2,954 yards and 22 touchdown passes. He finished sixth in the

Heisman Trophy voting. (The Heisman goes to the best player in college football.) Better yet, Tennessee finished the season ranked number 2 in the nation, according to the coaches' poll (they were number 3 in the Associated Press poll). The future was bright. With Peyton Manning at the helm, there was no telling what the Vols would be capable of in 1996.

Chapter Three

Upperclassman

Expectations were high entering the 1996 season. It was Peyton's junior season and possibly his last if he chose to enter the 1997 NFL draft. Many college football experts picked the Vols as the preseason favorite to win the national championship, and they were ranked number one entering the season. The team seemed to have the whole package—a strong, shut-down defense, a potent offense, and a true team leader at quarterback.

Still, Peyton knew that until the team played a game, it was all just hype. "Number one in the country sounds so good, but it's so much better after the season."

Everything started out according to plan with a 62–3 win over the University of Nevada, Las Vegas (UNLV). Tennessee got a scare in the second game, against UCLA, but Peyton's 53-yard touchdown pass to Kent sealed the victory, 35–20.

It was a win, but it wasn't quite what the fans, coaches, and players had been expecting. The top team in the nation should be winning games handily. So when Florida came to town in week three, everyone was understandably nervous. In Peyton's first two years with the team, Florida had wiped the floor with the Vols. Peyton and his teammates were eager for revenge. But could they finally beat the Gators?

The crowd was pumped up. Peyton led his team onto the field for what was, at the time, one of the biggest games of his life. Everyone expected a tight, hard-fought game. But the Gators silenced the crowd with a touchdown on their opening drive. It only got worse from there. Soon it was 14–0, then 21–0. The Tennessee crowd was all but silent as Florida erupted to a shocking 35–0 lead. Peyton had played terribly in the first half, throwing four interceptions. Nothing was going right.

Peyton and his teammates didn't give up, though. They rallied back in the second half, scoring 29 unanswered points. But it was too little, too late. They'd let Florida get off to far too large a lead. Even Peyton's 492 passing yards weren't enough to overcome the deficit.

The 35–29 Florida loss was tough to take, but Peyton couldn't dwell on it. Next up on the schedule was a game he'd been dreading for a long time—Tennessee at Ole Miss. What kind of greeting would the Mississippi fans give him? Peyton's visit was a huge story at Ole Miss. The media coverage was intense. Archie and Olivia left home to get away from all the reporters wanting to talk to them about the game.

> The Mannings had known all along that pitting Peyton against his dad's old team would cause a stir. When the Tennessee head coach had visited the Mannings on a recruiting visit several years before, Olivia asked him if the Vols would play Ole Miss. The coach lied and said no. He didn't want to dissuade Peyton from choosing Tennessee.

"I'd just as soon not deal with [the media]," Archie said. "I just don't plan to get in the middle of it. I know a lot of people want opinions on this or that. I don't plan to do that a hundred times."

Peyton knew that all eyes would be on him. "I sure didn't want to go down there in front of a lot of people watching me and just flop and play badly and lose, because I knew I'd never hear the end of it," he said.

Poor play wasn't a problem. Many of the fans were still angry and eager to let Peyton know it, but his performance quickly sucked the life out of the crowd. He went 18 of 22 for 242 yards and a touchdown as Tennessee rolled to a 41–3 victory. The twenty-year-old quarterback was glad to get a win, but he was even more relieved to get the game behind him.

The Volunteers kept rolling. They beat Georgia 29–17 in one of Peyton's best games. The highlight of the game came on one of the strangest plays of Peyton's career. Tennessee was on Georgia's 5-yard line. It was third down, and the Vols needed less than a yard for a fresh set of downs. Cutcliffe called a quarterback sneak. Peyton was supposed to carry the ball forward a yard, behind his surging offensive line. It should have been a simple play. But Georgia's defense came blasting through, and Peyton knew he wouldn't make it. So he ran backward. He drifted farther and farther back until he was at the 23-yard line—18 yards behind the line of scrimmage! Peyton frantically looked around, then finally saw receiver Marcus Nash downfield. He fired the ball toward the end zone. Nash made a fantastic catch as he was falling out of bounds—touchdown!

 Peyton's mad scramble against Georgia was nominated for an ESPY Award (a sports award given by ESPN) as college football's most bizarre moment of 1996.

"It's a play you laugh at," Peyton later said. "You can't do anything else but laugh. It'll never happen again in my career."

The thrills kept coming. In the next game, Tennessee trailed Alabama 13–0 in the second half but came back to win it in the fourth quarter. After yet another win, the Vols were 6–1. The next game, at in-state rival Memphis, didn't seem too threatening. Memphis was a heavy underdog, and Tennessee needed a win to secure a Bowl Alliance game (one of the top bowl games). But Peyton and his teammates played poorly and took a shocking 21–17 loss. It was one of the biggest upsets in Tennessee football history. Memphis had worked hard and played well. They deserved the victory. But by all accounts, Tennessee should not have lost to Memphis. The loss killed their hopes of getting into a Bowl Alliance game. And things just got worse the next week when Peyton strained his right knee. He didn't miss any games, but the injury slowed him down.

The Vols finished the season at 9–2. They returned to the Citrus Bowl and won it once again. Peyton dominated the Northwestern Wildcats, throwing for 408 yards and 4 touchdowns. As the clock's final second ticked down, the Tennessee fans in the stands stood and chanted, "One more year! One more year!" They were hoping Peyton would be back for his senior season.

The question of what Peyton would do was the talk of college football and the NFL. Pro scouts agreed that he'd almost certainly be the first overall pick if he chose to leave school early. And if that wasn't enough, Peyton's hard work in the classroom had earned him enough credits to graduate that spring. There seemed little reason for him not to turn pro.

But Peyton had one reason that nobody else seemed to have thought of—he loved college. And he desperately wanted to win a national championship. He talked to former stars of the NFL and other sports, asking for their advice. Troy Aikman, Michael Jordan, Roger Staubach, and Drew Bledsoe were just a few of the big names who helped Peyton make up his mind.

When he finally called a press conference on March 5, 1997, everyone was eager to know what he'd decided. Most of the 150 people attending the press conference assumed that Peyton was officially making himself eligible for the NFL draft later that spring.

"I made up my mind and I don't expect to ever look back," Peyton said calmly. "I am going to stay at the University of Tennessee."

With that—and the thunderous applause that followed—Tennessee fans were already looking ahead to the 1997 season. Peyton was the face of college football. He was on countless magazine covers. Newspaper and TV reporters clamored for interviews. He even did public service announcements telling kids to learn to read and to wear bicycle helmets. Everything seemed perfect.

❝ *I wanted to create more memories. Staying was strong in my mind and my heart, and that's what I wanted to do.*❞

—Peyton Manning

But just a few days before the season began, Peyton was in the headlines for a very different reason. The University of Tennessee had agreed to a settlement with a former athletic trainer. The woman had sued the school for numerous accounts of sexual harassment, including one incident involving Peyton. The trainer had been working on Peyton's ankle when Peyton had pulled down his pants to "moon" a friend. The problem was that the trainer was right there, and she felt hurt and insulted by Peyton's inappropriate behavior.

It was a rare bit of controversy for the usually clean-cut Peyton. He issued a public apology, but the woman refused it. She didn't believe that he had intended to moon a friend, as he claimed. The media kept talking about the incident, and it overshadowed much of the early part of the season.

On the field, things were going much better for the twenty-one-year-old quarterback. His five touchdown passes led the team to a win over Texas Tech, which was followed by a close victory over UCLA. Then the Vols took their 2–0 record to Florida for the biggest game of the year. Would this be the season for the Vols to break through against the Gators? The excitement was high building up to the game. But the result was familiar. Florida jumped to an early lead, which included a touchdown off an interception Peyton threw. The Gators handed Tennessee yet another loss, this time 33–20. Peyton's description of the game was simple: "It wasn't much fun."

In 1997 Peyton became the SEC's all-time passing leader with 11,201 yards. At the time, only two college quarterbacks (both in other conferences) had ever thrown for more.

Only three games into the season, another trip to the Citrus Bowl seemed likely. But the Vols rebounded from the Florida loss and started racking up the wins. Freshman running back Jamal Lewis teamed with Peyton for a lethal offensive combination. And when Florida lost in a shocker to Louisiana State, the Vols were right back in the hunt for an SEC title (conference championship).

The wins kept coming. Tennessee was 8–1 entering a game with Kentucky. The game featured the top two offenses in the SEC. As expected, the football was flying all over the field. Peyton set a school record with an amazing 523 passing yards. Tennessee won the shootout, 59–31. When they beat Auburn 30–29 two weeks later, they were the SEC champions!

Tennessee fans thought Peyton would be the 1997 Heisman winner. His 3,819 passing yards and 36 touchdowns were school records. But the award went to Michigan cornerback Charles Woodson. It was the first time a defensive player had won the Heisman.

With their SEC title, the third-ranked Vols were set to play in a Bowl Alliance game. The Bowl Alliance was set up to help college football determine a national champion. Ideally, the two top-ranked teams would face off against each other in a bowl game. The top two teams in 1997 were Nebraska and Michigan. But Michigan was the Big Ten conference champ, which always played the Pac-10 leader in the Rose Bowl. So Nebraska would play number 3, Tennessee, in the Orange Bowl. If Tennessee won and Michigan lost to Washington State in the Rose Bowl, the Vols would be the champs.

But headed into the Orange Bowl, that result seemed unlikely. Peyton had hurt his knee in the season's final game, against Auburn. The knee swelled up so badly that Peyton had to spend time in a hospital. He played in the Orange Bowl, but he wasn't himself, throwing for just 134 yards. Nebraska dominated the Vols and cruised to an easy 42–17 victory. Peyton's college football career was over.

"For me personally, [college] was an unbelievable experience," he said. "If I went back and did it again, I wouldn't change one thing." But college was in Peyton's past. The NFL was waiting.

Chapter Four

The Next Step

By most accounts, Peyton would have been the first overall pick in the 1997 draft if he'd chosen to leave Tennessee a year early. But even after his brilliant senior season, his status as the first overall pick in 1998 was in question. Washington State quarterback Ryan Leaf had also enjoyed a fine season in college. Leaf was six-foot five and had a cannon for an arm. Scouts agreed that, of the two quarterbacks, Peyton was more NFL ready. But many also believed that Leaf might be the man with more long-term potential. The fans and the media fiercely debated which quarterback the Indianapolis Colts should select with the top overall pick. One poll run by the *Indianapolis Star* revealed that more fans preferred Leaf to Manning.

The Colts had earned the first pick by being the NFL's worst team in 1997. The team had been bad for a long time and was ready to start over with a new quarterback. Both Peyton and

Leaf had private workouts for Colts' officials. The Colts reportedly couldn't make up their minds.

"I think [Colts' owner Jim Irsay] liked me," Peyton later wrote. "I know I liked him. So as I was leaving, I said, 'You know, Mr. Irsay, I'll win for you.'"

That simple, confident statement made a big impact on Irsay. So when the Colts announced their selection on April 18, it was Peyton Manning. Even Leaf, who was scooped up second by the San Diego Chargers, admitted that Peyton deserved to be first. "What else does [Peyton] have to prove?" Leaf said.

Peyton, meanwhile, was thrilled. "I'm excited about getting started and playing," he said. "This is a special day in my life, and I can promise the franchise and the city that they are getting a player who will dedicate everything he has to the game."

That summer, shortly after training camp started, Peyton and the Colts agreed to a contract. The six-year deal was worth a total of $38 million, with incentives (bonuses) that could push up the value another $10 million. It was the richest rookie contract in the history of the league. In addition, Peyton could earn income on the side by endorsing products in advertisements. At age twenty-two, Peyton was already a very wealthy young man.

The money didn't change him, though. According to Archie, Peyton didn't rush out to buy expensive foreign cars and huge mansions. After he signed the contract, he made only one big purchase. He bought a fancy cowboy hat for $200 while on vacation in Wyoming.

Peyton was once asked what he planned to do with all the money that his contract would pay him. His answer was simple: "Earn it."

The money was nice. Peyton could afford a comfortable home. He and his girlfriend, Ashley, could go out for nice dinners. But for Peyton, it was all about football. Peyton picked jersey number 18—Archie's number in college—and hit the practice fields with his teammates. He felt comfortable from the beginning. Head coach Jim Mora and the Colts showed nothing but confidence in him. They knew he would struggle at first. But the Colts had been terrible for a long time, and there was little pressure to succeed right away. His rookie season was to be mostly a learning experience.

The Colts' first preseason game of 1998 was against the Seattle Seahawks. Peyton was still rough around the edges, but he gave Indy fans a reason to smile. His first pass went to receiver Marvin Harrison for a 48-yard touchdown. Colts fans hoped it was just the start of a great quarterback-receiver relationship between the two young stars.

Finally, opening day arrived. Mora formally announced that Peyton would be the starter, despite the protests of some fans and reporters who said it was unfair to start the rookie. Mora explained that the Colts were committed to the rookie quarterback and that they hadn't drafted him first to let him sit on the bench.

"I think that if you're a quarterback . . . you want that kind of pressure," Peyton said. "You want to be in that situation where they're counting on you to win some games. All I know how to do . . . is go in and work hard and study [as] hard as I possibly can. It is a lot of pressure, but it's something I'm looking forward to trying [to] handle."

❝ You are my starting quarterback, no matter what. We have that kind of faith in you. But I don't want you to think I'm doing you any favors. I'm actually doing you an injustice, because you're a rookie and it's going to be tough on you. But we feel for the future of this team that the way for you to get better as quickly as possible is to play. Experience will be your best teacher. ❞

—COLTS COACH JIM MORA TO PEYTON
BEFORE HIS ROOKIE SEASON

The Miami Dolphins and future Hall of Fame quarterback Dan Marino were the Colts' opponents in the opener. It was, in a way, the passing of the torch. Marino was perhaps the finest passing quarterback of the 1980s and 1990s, while Peyton hoped to go on to become the best passing quarterback of the 2000s.

The Dolphins blitzed (sent extra pass rushers at the quarterback) on the Colts' first offensive play. It was a tactic Peyton had expected. Most defenses like to try to rattle young quarterbacks. Peyton saw the blitz coming and remained calm. He made a quick, short pass to running back Marshall Faulk. Faulk caught the ball and charged forward for a 20-yard gain. The Indianapolis crowd roared—it was an encouraging start.

But the highlights that day were few and far between. The Colts quickly fell behind, and Peyton threw 3 interceptions in a 24–15 loss. His first touchdown pass was a meaningless last-minute toss to Harrison.

Any fans who had hoped that young Peyton would instantly transform the Colts into a contender were in for a rude awakening. The Colts lost their first four games. And they weren't just losing, they were getting steamrolled. Peyton was giving his all, but his inexperience showed.

After one of the losses, Peyton was watching the game tapes. He was studying his own plays, breaking down what he'd done well and what he'd done poorly. Archie had always told him that after a bad game, you were never as bad as you thought. Peyton called his dad to correct him. "You know, Dad, that part about it never being as bad as you think? Guess what. It was worse."

---

66 *It's not fun, not at all. You're not going to accept losing and you never want to get used to losing. . . . All we can do is learn from it. I have the same goals every week: that's just to win the game, no matter how I play or my numbers, do whatever it takes to win. When you lose, as the quarterback, you feel like you didn't do your job. All you can do is keep working.* 99

—PEYTON, FOLLOWING A 44–6 LOSS
EARLY IN HIS ROOKIE SEASON

There was no time for self-pity, though. Many Colts fans had circled the season's fifth game on their schedules. The Colts were set to face the Chargers and Ryan Leaf. Most fans knew that they had to be patient with Peyton. But others were frustrated with his poor performance and continued to question why the Colts hadn't selected Leaf. The fact that Leaf's Chargers had already won two games didn't help matters. Peyton was, after all, supposed to be the more NFL-ready quarterback. The game would give fans a chance to compare the two young players. While neither Peyton nor Leaf played particularly well in the game, the Colts finally notched their first win of the season, 17–12. The win didn't end the talk about Leaf entirely, but it did a lot to quiet the Leaf supporters.

RYAN LEAF

Ryan Leaf had been a college football star at Washington State. He was third in the 1997 Heisman Trophy voting, just behind Peyton. Many considered him a can't-miss prospect who should be drafted ahead of Peyton, and he was drafted second overall by the Chargers. But Leaf never adjusted to the NFL game. He struggled on the field and couldn't manage his sharp temper off it. He served mainly as a backup for the Chargers, Buccaneers, Cowboys, and Seahawks until 2002, when he retired. He later went into coaching.

The win was one of only a handful of highlights in a long rookie season. Another came against the New York Jets, when Peyton led his offense to a last-minute, game-winning touchdown. The 80-yard drive ended with a 14-yard touchdown pass to tight end Marcus Pollard. By season's end, the Colts record stood at 3–13—identical to the team's record the previous season. It had been a difficult learning experience for Peyton. He wasn't used to losing. The fact that he set NFL rookie records for touchdowns (26), passing yards (3,739), and completions (326) was little consolation. He was also named to the NFL's All-Rookie Team and was the only quarterback in the league to take every one of his team's offensive snaps.

"Winning three games, that's not good enough, no matter how young you are or what kind of team you have," Peyton said of the season. "We know that and I think . . . everybody's got kind of a sour taste in their mouth."

A MINOR CONTROVERSY

Late in his rookie season, after a loss, Peyton was asked about the Tennessee Volunteers, who were having a great season. But Peyton, still frustrated about the loss, was in no mood to talk about college football. "I'm really not thinking about that right now," he snapped. The quote set off a minor controversy, with people saying that Peyton didn't care about his old teammates. But Peyton hadn't meant that. He'd just been so focused on a disappointing loss that he didn't want to talk about another team.

The season was over, but Peyton wasn't about to rest. He never wanted to endure another 3–13 season. He worked out, determined to report to training camp better than ever. He practiced his timing and his footwork. He worked on his release of the football. He even practiced with his receivers—especially Harrison. Like Peyton, Harrison was a hard worker who was willing to do what it took to turn the Colts into a winning team.

Meanwhile, the Colts' front office was working to get Peyton some help on the field. They had a high draft pick in 1999 and used it on University of Miami running back Edgerrin James. They hoped that with Harrison and James, Peyton would be able to take the Colts' offense to new heights.

Chapter Five

Turning It Around

In the summer of 1999, Peyton showed up to training camp ready to go. He couldn't wait to get back onto the field and erase the memory of the 1998 season. He was stronger, smarter, and more experienced than he'd been the previous year. The Colts were undeniably his team. The team was young, but it was also confident.

Before the first game, against the Buffalo Bills, Peyton gathered his teammates. He made it clear to them that he wasn't going to settle for losing. "We're not going 3 and 13 this year. We're better. We've worked hard. Let's stay together, be positive, get a fast start. Have a killer instinct."

Peyton was right. The Colts were no longer one of the league's worst teams. He completed 21 of 33 passes against the Bills, racking up 284 yards and 2 touchdowns. The Colts won easily, 31–14. For the first time in years, Colts fans had a real reason to be excited. After the game, Peyton went out with Archie, Olivia, and Ashley to celebrate.

The Colts stumbled a little bit after the first game, though. They suffered a tough loss to the New England Patriots the next week. After holding a 28–7 lead (built with three Manning-to-Harrison touchdown passes), the Colts stumbled, bumbled, and fumbled their way to a heartbreaking 31–28 loss.

GOAL ORIENTED

Peyton believes in setting and achieving goals. Before the 1999 season, he made a list of his personal and team goals. "An athlete has to have goals—for a day, for a lifetime," he later wrote. "I like to put mine in writing so that afterward I can check the design against the finished product."

After a win against the Chargers, in which Peyton passed for a Colt record 404 yards, the Colts lost 34–31 to Marino and the Dolphins. The Colts were 2–2, which was still a big improvement over recent years. But Peyton expected better.

When the Colts and Jets took the field for the season's fifth game, few NFL fans suspected that the game would be the start of anything special. It was a defensive battle that the Colts pulled out, 16–13. Peyton didn't have a great game, despite the win. But the almost-forgettable victory was the beginning of a winning streak that nobody had seen coming. The Colts won their next game, then the one after that. Their offense seemed unstoppable at times. The Triplets—Peyton, Harrison, and James—were tearing apart opposing defenses.

MARVIN HARRISON

Marvin Harrison was born August 25, 1972, in Philadelphia, Pennsylvania. He played for Syracuse University before the Colts drafted him in the first round of the 1996 draft. Harrison stands just six feet tall—small by standards for NFL receivers—but his hard work, good hands, and precise route running have made him one of the NFL's all-time great receivers. His finest individual season may have been 2002, when he broke the NFL's record for receptions in a season, catching 143 passes for 1,722 yards and 11 touchdowns.

The Colts' record grew to 6–2. A playoff spot was starting to look realistic. By December, the team had won seven games in a row. They put that streak on the line against the division-leading Dolphins in Miami. Could they really hope to win on the road against the powerful Dolphins?

The Colts jumped out to an early lead, outscoring the Dolphins 17–3 in the first quarter. But Miami fought back. With less than a minute to play in the fourth quarter, the Dolphins kicked a field goal to tie the game, 34–34. Only 36 seconds remained on the clock when the Colts got the ball back at their own 31-yard line. The Colts could play it safe and go into overtime. Or they could try to get into kicker Mike Vanderjagt's field-goal range for a game-winning attempt. Peyton and the Colts went for the win. He calmly directed the hurry-up offense and connected with Harrison for two passes. Vanderjagt came onto the field and kicked the game winner as the final second ticked off the clock. The Colts had done it! It was easily Peyton's biggest win so far as a professional.

And the season just got better. Two weeks later, the Colts extended the streak to 10 games with a 24–21 win over the Washington Redskins. The Redskins led the game at halftime, but Peyton's one-yard touchdown pass to tight end Ken Dilger helped seal the win for Indy. When the final whistle blew, Peyton and the Colts had yet another reason to celebrate. They had clinched the American Football Conference (AFC) East title! With two games left in the season, they'd already secured a playoff spot and exceeded all expectations.

"It's been a fast turnaround," Peyton said after the Washington victory. "It's definitely come faster than we expected. We knew we'd be a better football team this year, but we didn't know that we'd be this good."

Indianapolis pushed the winning streak to 11 games before losing the season's last game to Buffalo. Their amazing winning streak had propelled them to a 13–3 record, giving them the biggest turnaround in NFL history. Peyton led the way with 4,135 yards and 26 touchdowns. His tremendous performance earned him his first selection to the NFL's Pro Bowl (all-star game). Even better, both Harrison and James would be joining him for the game!

Pro Bowl

Each year the AFC's biggest stars face off against the NFC's best in the Pro Bowl, held in Hawaii the week after the Super Bowl. Coaches, players, and fans vote to choose the players on each team. Peyton has been selected almost every year since his first Pro Bowl in 2000 (following the 1999 season). In the 2008 Pro Bowl, his eighth, he was the game's leading passer.

But first, the Colts had some work to do. Indy fans were buzzing with excitement about the playoffs. Could a team that had gone 3–13 in each of its last two seasons really be a Super Bowl contender? They couldn't wait to find out.

The Colts had earned a first-round bye (week off). So they watched the Wild Card round of the playoffs to find out who they'd be playing. They saw the Tennessee Titans beat the Bills on one of the most exciting plays in NFL history—a last-second kickoff return for the game-winning touchdown. The thrilling win meant that the Colts would be facing a Titans team brimming with confidence in the divisional round of the AFC playoffs.

The Indianapolis crowd was excited and noisy during the game's first half. It was a defensive game—exactly what the Titans wanted. The Colts drove the ball well but couldn't get into the end zone. Their three field goals sent them into halftime with a 9–6 lead. They felt good about the lead but knew that they'd need to do better if they wanted to stay ahead.

The Titans took the lead in the second half and didn't look back. Peyton played poorly against the strong Tennessee defense. His offensive line wasn't blocking well, and he was under constant pressure. He threw for just 19 of 43 in the game, and even a late touchdown wasn't enough. The Titans won the game 19–16. Just like that, the Colts' season was over.

The ending may have been a letdown for the Indy faithful, but on the whole it had been an amazing season—a success by any reasonable measure. In just one year, the Colts had gone from a perennial doormat to a Super Bowl favorite.

Peyton wasn't the only Manning enjoying success, however. His little brother, Eli, had wrapped up a fine high school career in 1999 and was a heavily recruited quarterback. Peyton's old offensive coordinator and friend, David Cutcliffe, had taken the head coaching job at Ole Miss, and Eli accepted a scholarship to play there, following in Archie's footsteps. It was a great fit for Eli.

Peyton enjoyed watching Eli, but his attention was focused squarely on the Colts. Their success in 1999 had built up expectations for the team. Many football experts believed that the Colts would be among the NFL's best teams in 2000. At first, it seemed that the experts might be right. The team started the season red-hot, winning six of its first eight games, often by wide margins. Most memorable was a 43–14 blowout of the Jacksonville Jaguars on *Monday Night Football,* in which Manning set a Colts record with 440 passing yards. But problems were developing. The team's defense often struggled badly. The offense was better than ever, but it constantly battled to make up for the poor defensive play.

The inconsistent play soon caught up with Indianapolis. Week after week, the same scenario played out: the Triplets doing all they could to erase a big lead given up by the defense. Sometimes, they succeeded. But other times, they just couldn't do enough. The team's record fell to 7–6, and the playoffs were very much in doubt. It took a season-ending three-game winning streak to propel the team to a berth in the playoffs as a Wild Card. Earning a playoff spot was big, but the final 10–6 mark was a disappointment for a team that had expected to be among the league's best. Still, they were in the playoffs. All they had to do was find their rhythm and the struggles in the regular season would be forgotten.

The team traveled to Miami for the Wild Card round. The defensive-minded Dolphins, who had edged out the Colts for the AFC East title, would be focused on stopping Peyton. Early on, the Colts seemed to be on their way to a playoff victory. They took a 14–0 lead into halftime, highlighted by a 17-yard touchdown pass from Peyton to Jerome Pathon. The offense was faring well against the tough Miami defense. And the Colts' defense had even held up against the Miami offense, led by quarterback Jay Fiedler. (Dan Marino had retired after the 1999 season.) Were the Colts on their way to their first playoff victory with Peyton?

It wasn't to be. Everything fell apart for Indianapolis in the second half. Miami came back to tie the game 17–17 in the final minute of regulation. The Colts still had a chance to win it in overtime. Peyton led the team down the field and set up a field-goal attempt, but the kick was no good. On the next Dolphin drive, Miami running back Lamar Smith scampered for a

17-yard touchdown that sent the Colts home empty-handed once again.

Peyton put the blame for the loss on his own shoulders. "Everybody is just frustrated," he said. "Looking back at it now, there were just a lot of missed opportunities. We got field goals and didn't get touchdowns."

In the 2001 draft, the Colts shocked their fans by drafting another offensive player, wide receiver Reggie Wayne, in the first round. Fans were upset that the front office was doing little to improve the team's porous defense.

It was a tough end to a disappointing season. Twenty-five-year-old Peyton couldn't be upset for long, though. He had a lot to be happy about, especially his wedding to Ashley a few months later.

He was soon back at work to improve in the 2001 season. Most people saw the Colts as a team on the rise. With back-to-back playoff appearances, it seemed only a matter of time before they were a dominating force in the league.

The 2001 season started out fine. The Colts dominated their first two games, winning by a combined score of 87–50. But the team's bad defense hadn't improved. If anything, it had gotten worse. And James was sidelined with a knee injury in the sixth game, increasing the pressure on Peyton and Harrison. The two stars did their best, but it wasn't even close to enough. After the 2–0 start, the team lost 10 of its last 14 games. Peyton was embarrassed by the team's 6–10 record. It was bad enough losing playoff games. Not making the playoffs at all was even worse.

Chapter Six

A New Regime

In the NFL, coaches usually take the fall when a team fails to live up to expectations. So it was little surprise that Mora was fired after the miserable 2001 season. The Colts hired former Tampa Bay coach Tony Dungy to turn things around. Dungy was respected around the league as a brilliant defensive mind. He had built strong defenses with the Minnesota Vikings as a defensive coordinator and with Tampa Bay as the head coach. His defensive specialty seemed like a perfect fit for the Colts.

"I really like him," Peyton said of his new head coach. "I think we're kind of in similar situations, both used to success and having last year not going the way we wanted. I really don't like to get into comparisons with him and Coach Mora, but I've gotten to know Tony and he's a pretty player-friendly coach. At the same time, we're still getting the same quality of work done. It's just a good setup."

TONY DUNGY

Tony Dungy was born October 6, 1955, in Jackson, Michigan. Dungy played quarterback at the University of Minnesota and then played for the Pittsburgh Steelers, though he switched to defensive back. He won a Super Bowl with the Steelers after the 1978 season. After retiring as a player, Dungy took a job as Pittsburgh's defensive backs coach. He was also a defensive coordinator for the Steelers and Vikings before becoming the head coach at Tampa Bay. He is famous for his "Tampa 2" defense, designed to prevent long pass completions.

The coaching switch led to mixed results in 2002. Nobody—not even Dungy—could be expected to fix the Colts' defense overnight, and James was still battling injuries. The pressure to carry the team rested squarely on Peyton's shoulders. He was up to the challenge more often than not. The Colts started hot again, going 3–1 to start the season. But old problems soon resurfaced. The Colts' defense wasn't able to match the intensity of the team's potent offense, and Indy's record dropped to 4–4. Once again, it was looking like the Colts might miss the playoffs entirely.

The ninth game was in Philadelphia against the powerful Eagles. The Colts were heavy underdogs. On paper, the Eagles were the better team, and they were playing in their home stadium. But for once, both the Colts' offense and defense were up to the challenge. Peyton and the offense were moving the ball up and down the field, and the defense was shutting down the Eagles' offense. Peyton was nearly perfect in the game, throwing 3 touchdown passes and posting the highest-possible passer rating of 158.3. (The passer rating is a statistic that measures a quarterback's overall effectiveness.) In the end, the Colts surprised the Eagles—and the NFL—with a convincing 35–13 thrashing of Philadelphia.

The win turned the season around. The Colts lost only two more games that year to finish at 10–6, good enough for a Wild Card spot in the AFC playoffs.

Peyton, 0–2 in playoff games, was battling criticism from fans and reporters who said he couldn't win a big game (despite his good bowl record at Tennessee). Peyton would have a chance to silence those critics if he could lead the team to a victory over the New York Jets, their Wild Card game opponent. The two teams appeared to be pretty well matched, and the game looked like it would be close. This was Peyton's best chance yet to get a playoff win.

But once again, the plan didn't work out. The Jets jumped to an early lead and just kept pouring it on. Few fans were surprised to see the Indy defense struggle, but nobody was prepared to see Peyton and the offense flounder so badly. Peyton was awful in the game. He completed just 14 of 31 passes for a paltry 137 yards. Losing yet another playoff game was bad enough, but the final score of 41–0 was a complete embarrassment. Fans, reporters, and even fellow teammates said that Peyton had choked under the pressure. Worst of all, who would argue with them? Were Peyton's critics right? Was he just a good regular-season quarterback who didn't have the mental strength to perform in the playoffs?

"I'm a pretty wide-open target," Peyton said of the familiar criticism. "All I can do is sit here and take it. I'm fully responsible when we don't win. . . . I understand how the system works."

Peyton was no quitter, though. He knew he had only one way to silence his critics. He had to win in the playoffs. And the only way to do that was to return to training camp in the summer of 2003 and start over.

The Colts jumped out to another encouraging start. They won their first three games, highlighted by a 33–7 dismantling of the Titans. James was finally healthy again, and Peyton was clicking with his receivers—especially Harrison. The Colts kept rolling in the fourth game, against the Saints. Peyton was on fire against his dad's old team, throwing for a jaw-dropping 6 touchdowns in a 55–21 win.

The Colts took their 4–0 record onto *Monday Night Football* in week five. It was one of the season's most intriguing matchups. The league's best offense in the Colts was up against the best defense, the Tampa Bay Buccaneers. Dungy's old team had won the Super Bowl in their first year after his departure. The game promised to be one of Indy's biggest tests of the year. But with just 6 minutes to play in the fourth quarter, the Colts were trailing by 14 points and were backed up deep in their own territory. Peyton dropped back and tried to thread a pass over the middle. But Tampa's Ronde Barber intercepted the pass and ran it back for a touchdown.

With an almost insurmountable 35–14 lead, the Bucs and their fans were celebrating a big win. Peyton, meanwhile, wasn't ready to accept defeat. He prepared to take the field once again. "I never lost confidence," Peyton said. "But I'm not going to lie, it didn't look good."

Peyton and his offense took the ball and marched down the field. With less than 4 minutes left in the game, they were at Tampa's 3-yard line. Peyton handed off the ball to running back James Mungro, who rushed ahead for a touchdown. Wasting no time, the Colts then recovered an onside kick (a short kick that either team can recover) to get the ball back. Peyton led another frantic drive. This time, the Colts needed just over a minute to strike again. Peyton found Harrison down the sideline for a

28-yard touchdown pass. Suddenly, the lead was trimmed to just 7 points.

The Tampa offense wasn't able to do much with their next possession. The Colts forced a punt, and the offense took the field once again. Peyton wasted no time. He hit Troy Walters with a short pass, then connected with Harrison on a 52-yard pass that brought the Colts to Tampa's 5-yard line. On the next play, running back Ricky Williams punched it into the end zone, completing the comeback. The Colts had scored 3 touchdowns in less than 4 minutes to erase a 21-point deficit!

After such a historic comeback, the Colts were determined not to lose in overtime. They held their momentum, and Vanderjagt won the game on a 39-yard field goal, completing what may have been the most improbable comeback in NFL history.

"I tip my hat to Manning," said a disgusted Jon Gruden, Tampa's coach, after the game. "He made some miraculous throws, and they made some incredible catches."

Everything was coming together. Peyton had a 5–0 record to go along with his gaudy statistics. The buzz around the league was that he was one of the top candidates for the NFL's Most Valuable Player (MVP) award. But Peyton knew that individual honors didn't matter. Even if he won the award, he wouldn't get the respect he deserved until he performed in the playoffs.

The winning streak was snapped the next week with an overtime loss to the Carolina Panthers. The Colts went on to finish the season 12–4, good enough for the AFC South title. And after the regular season, the NFL announced that Peyton and Tennessee quarterback Steve McNair were the league's co-MVPs. Peyton had thrown for 4,267 yards and 29 touchdowns in his finest season so far.

In 2002 the NFL realigned the league, going from six divisions to eight. As part of the change, the Colts were moved from the AFC East to the newly created AFC South.

Things just got better after that. Peyton, Dungy, and the Colts finally shed the label of playoff losers with their 41–10 blowout of the Denver Broncos in the Wild Card round. Next up was a trip to Kansas City to play the Chiefs. The Chiefs had entered the season as the AFC favorite, but they suffered from the same problems that had plagued the Colts for years. Their weak defense couldn't support their powerful offense.

This game would clearly be a high-scoring affair. Peyton and the Colts traded score after score with the Chiefs' offense.

The offenses were so good, and the defenses so bad, that for the first time in the history of the NFL playoffs, neither team punted even once. But Peyton and the Colts were just a little bit better than the Chiefs. Late in the third quarter, Peyton hit Wayne for a 19-yard touchdown—Peyton's third of the day—to give the Colts a 31–17 lead, and they held on for a 38–31 victory. The victory sent them to the AFC Championship Game, just one step from the Super Bowl!

"I am hot right now, we're hot as an offense," Peyton said after his performance. "It's not trickery, just running the same plays we've run all season. Hopefully, we can keep it up next week."

Standing between the Colts and the Super Bowl were the defending Super Bowl champs, the New England Patriots, led by quarterback Tom Brady. Most people considered Brady and Manning to be the two best young quarterbacks in the league, and a rivalry between them was beginning to grow. The biggest difference between them, at least that year, was that Brady's Patriots had a great defense to go along with a good offense. That difference ended up being key.

The Patriots ended Indy's season with a 24–14 victory. The New England defense confused and frustrated Peyton and his receivers all day. Peyton threw four interceptions and took most of the blame for the loss.

Ironically, even after winning two playoff games that season, the questions about Peyton's ability to come through in the big game resurfaced. It was becoming clear that nothing short of a Super Bowl victory would completely silence Peyton's critics.

Chapter Seven

Rewriting the Record Books

In March 2004, Peyton and the Colts' management agreed to a seven-year contract extension worth more than $98 million—at the time, the richest contract in NFL history. So when the 2004 season came around, Peyton was eager to earn his money. The 2004 regular season would be one for the ages for twenty-eight-year-old Peyton. The opener was in New England, a rematch of the AFC title game. Manning vs. Brady was, for the NFL, a marketing dream. Could Peyton and the Colts get revenge on the Patriots? Peyton did all he could, and during the game he reached a personal milestone with 25,000 career passing yards. But it wasn't enough. Once again, Brady, backed by a stout defense, got the better of the matchup with a 27–24 victory.

The Colts quickly got back on track with wins over the Titans and the Green Bay Packers. Peyton's 5 touchdown passes against Green Bay gave him a total of 9 through just 3 games.

Peyton Manning talks to his dad, Archie, after a Tennessee win in 1995.

During his senior year at Tennessee, Peyton Manning won the Johnny Unitas Golden Arm Award and ring, given to outstanding senior quarterbacks. Hall of Fame quarterback Johnny Unitas himself presented the award to Peyton.

Peyton Manning holds up his new jersey at the 1998 NFL Draft, where he was drafted first overall by the Indianapolis Colts.

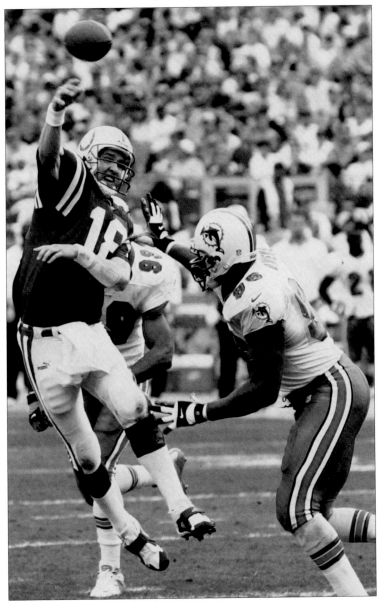

Peyton throws a pass under pressure during the December 1999 Colts-Dolphins game in Miami. The Colts pulled out a landmark win.

Colts head coach Tony Dungy talks with Peyton Manning on the sideline during a 2003 game against the Buffalo Bills.

On January 4, 2004, Peyton Manning proved he could win in the playoffs. Here he throws a pass in the AFC Wild Card game against the Denver Broncos, his first playoff victory.

Peyton and his wife, Ashley *(second from left)*, helped celebrate when Eli Manning was picked first overall in the 2004 NFL Draft. Also present were Olivia Manning *(third from left)*; Eli's girlfriend (now wife), Abby McGrew *(third from right)*; and Archie Manning.

Peyton Manning drops back in the pocket to throw his 49th touchdown pass of the 2004 season, caught by Brandon Stokley. Peyton broke Dan Marino's record of 48 in this game against the San Diego Chargers on December 26.

Peyton greets a six-year-old boy at the Children's Hospital of Michigan in 2006. He often makes hospital visits as a way to give back to the community.

Peyton Manning and Colts coach Tony Dungy receive the Lombardi Trophy after winning Super Bowl XLI against the Chicago Bears on February 4, 2007. Peyton was named the Super Bowl MVP.

At that rate of 3 touchdown passes per game, Peyton was on pace to tie what was then the single-season record—48, held by Dan Marino. Even better, Peyton wasn't throwing interceptions. Many experts look at a quarterback's touchdown-to-interception ratio as a measure of success. Peyton's numbers in that regard were stellar. After eight games, his ratio stood at 26:4 (26 touchdown passes, 4 interceptions). That was almost impossibly good.

On September 9, 2004, Peyton got his 25,000th career passing yard in the 97th game of his career. Only Dan Marino reached that plateau faster.

During one five-game stretch in the middle of the season, Peyton threw 24 touchdown passes—almost 5 per game! The talk about him challenging Marino's record was really heating up. But Peyton insisted that he wasn't interested in the record. It was all about winning. "For us, just the total points is what I'm happy about," he said after throwing 5 touchdowns against the Houston Texans on November 14. "It's not something we're being conscious of as far as throwing touchdowns."

Peyton's chase for the record was getting most of the headlines. But the Colts were also battling for a playoff spot. The defense had been worse than ever at the beginning of the season. However, it improved a little late in the year, and suddenly the Colts looked dangerous. With only two games to play, the team had locked up a playoff spot. The real drama was whether Peyton would break Marino's record. After 14 games, he had 47 touchdown passes. He needed just two more to surpass Marino's mark.

Dan Marino

Experts frequently compare Peyton to the great Dan Marino. Their careers have a lot in common. Born September 15, 1961, in Pittsburgh, Pennsylvania, Marino was drafted by the Miami Dolphins in 1983. He was an instant success. He set his single-season record of 48 touchdown passes in 1984, just his second year in the pros. Marino led the Dolphins to the Super Bowl that season, but they lost to the San Francisco 49ers, 38–16. It was the only Super Bowl appearance of a long, successful career. He took the Dolphins to the playoffs in 10 of his 17 seasons before retiring after the 1999 season. Marino was elected to the Pro Football Hall of Fame in 2005.

On December 26, the Colts took the field at the RCA Dome to face the San Diego Chargers. The crowd was electric. They could sense that they were about to witness NFL history. But to their great disappointment, Peyton didn't throw a touchdown pass in the first half. Worse still, the Colts had fallen behind.

Peyton came back strong in the second half, throwing his record-tying 48th touchdown pass to running back James Mungro. The crowd went wild. But the game was still very much in doubt. As the final minutes of the fourth quarter ticked down, the Colts trailed by 8 points and the Indy fans were getting nervous. What if Peyton didn't break the record? What if the heavily favored Colts lost the game?

The Colts had the ball on their own 20-yard line. They had to drive 80 yards to their own end zone, then make a 2-point conversion just to get into overtime. It didn't look good. But Peyton was calm. He used a series of pinpoint passes to move closer and closer to the end zone. With about a minute to play, the Colts were still 21 yards away.

The coaches called in a play. But Peyton had other ideas. He ignored the play and told receiver Brandon Stokley to run a post route, straight down the center of the field. Peyton stepped to the line and barked signals to his offense. He took the snap and dropped back. He saw Stokley fake a route to the sideline, causing his defender to stumble. Peyton stepped forward and fired a rocket right into Stokley's hands. Touchdown number 49! The record was Peyton's!

The crowd went nuts, but on the field, Peyton knew that there was no time for a celebration. The Colts still trailed by 2 points. They needed to make the 2-point conversion to force overtime. Peyton didn't want the record-breaking pass to come in a losing effort. What fun would that be? He couldn't ever be happy about losing, even if he had just broken one of the NFL's greatest records.

The Colts had been throwing the ball consistently against the Chargers in the second half. They knew that the Charger defense would be expecting yet another pass. So they decided to use that to their advantage. Peyton took the snap and dropped back, as if he was going to throw the ball. But instead he handed it off to James in a delayed running play called a draw. The strategy worked perfectly, fooling the Charger defenders. James easily rushed forward into the end zone to tie the game. Overtime!

The stadium was noisier than ever. Between the touchdown record and the thrilling comeback, the fans were in a frenzy. Peyton didn't let the officials stop the game for a ceremony. He wanted to get the win first, then celebrate with his teammates.

A good day got even better in overtime as the Colts completed the comeback. Peyton led the team on a 61-yard drive that set up the 30-yard, game-winning field goal from Vanderjagt.

After the game, Peyton talked about the record breaker. "At the time I threw [the pass], there wasn't a lot of emotion for me, because if we don't get the two-point conversion, this is a down locker room right now. The fact that it happened, we won the game . . . it sure made for an exciting day."

After losing a relatively meaningless final regular-season game, the Colts headed into the playoffs. They had plenty of reasons to be optimistic. Their 12–4 record had earned them a home game in the Wild Card round. And after the season, Peyton had once again been voted the league's MVP.

The Broncos came to Indianapolis hoping to avenge their playoff loss from the previous year. But the end result was much the same. The Colts dominated the Broncos in every phase of the game for a 49–24 win. From the first snap, Peyton was in total control. He saw a rookie defender, Roc Alexander, lined up against Reggie Wayne. Peyton and Wayne exploited Alexander's inexperience time after time. The Broncos were helpless to stop the potent Colt passing attack. Peyton racked up 360 passing yards in the first half alone! By game's end, he had completed 27 of 33 passes for 457 yards— at the time, the second-highest playoff total in NFL history— and 4 touchdowns.

John Lynch, a safety for the Broncos, was dejected after the game. "This is the best offense I have ever played against," he told reporters. "I have never been in a game where so much has felt almost hopeless."

ORGANIZED CHAOS

Peyton may be best known for his frantic play calling at the line of scrimmage. Most quarterbacks call plays in a huddle. But Peyton barks out signals to his offense while standing at the line. He points, shifts, and orders his offense around. All the while, he is studying the defense, looking for weaknesses. It's a system that always looks a little out of control. But it allows Peyton to see what the defense wants to do and call a play that can exploit it.

Peyton was pleased by the convincing win, but he reminded everyone that it was just one game. "We want to win the whole thing," he said. "That's what I want to do. Obviously, individually, I've accomplished a lot, but I haven't been to the Super Bowl. . . . We've got a shot and that's all you can ask for."

Indy's reward for the big win was a rematch with the Patriots in New England. It was a blustery, cold day, and the Patriots were well prepared for Peyton's frantic passing game. New England started by employing a heavy running strategy. By running the ball, the Patriots went on long, clock-eating drives.

They kept Peyton, Harrison, and James on the sidelines. And when the Colts did get the ball, the Patriots' pressing, physical defense dominated the Colts. The NFL's best offense went out with a whimper, managing just a lonely field goal in a crushing 20–3 loss. Once again, the Colts were no match for New England. And after such a terrible performance, questions about Peyton's ability to win big games resurfaced.

"It was an excellent run, a fine year," Peyton said after the loss. "But when you finish with a loss in the playoffs, you can't be happy about it."

ELI COMES TO THE NFL

At Ole Miss, Eli Manning became one of the best college quarterbacks in the nation. He was the first overall pick in the 2004 NFL draft. The San Diego Chargers selected Eli, then immediately traded him to the New York Giants. Eli started out as the backup in New York but was the team's starter by midseason.

Once again, it was back to square one. Another promising start had ended in a poor playoff showing. Could the Colts rebound from yet another disappointment? Early on in the 2005 season, they had cause for concern. The team lost all five of its preseason games. Normally preseason games don't matter much, but losing all of them raised some eyebrows around the league. Were the Colts done as a Super Bowl contender?

Peyton and his teammates answered that question with a resounding no. Their regular season got off to another sizzling start, beginning with a 24–7 opening-day win over the Baltimore Ravens. The biggest difference between the 2005 Colts and past teams was its defense. Led by star defensive end Dwight Freeney, the Colts defense was finally up to the task of helping the offense win games. For the first time, it seemed, the Colts didn't have to score 30 points to have a chance, as evidenced by the team's 10–3 win over Jacksonville in the second game.

The wins kept coming. When the Colts took the field against the St. Louis Rams for *Monday Night Football* on October 17, Indy was 5–0. The team was looking to stay undefeated, but fans had another reason to be interested in the nationally televised game. In their eight seasons together, Peyton and Harrison had combined for 85 touchdown passes, tying them with San Francisco's Steve Young and Jerry Rice as the most prolific quarterback-receiver combination in NFL history. Could they break the record under the lights against the Rams?

At first, it didn't look good. The Rams, who also had a powerful offense, jumped out to a 17–0 lead. But Peyton and the

Colts came storming back. The highlight of the night came in the fourth quarter, when the Colts were driving at the St. Louis 6-yard line. Peyton took the snap and dropped back. Harrison, meanwhile, had faked his defender toward the inside of the field and broke for the back corner of the end zone. Peyton knew exactly where his favorite wide receiver wanted the ball. He lofted a high, slow pass that sailed over Harrison's shoulder and into his hands. The receiver dragged his feet in bounds for the touchdown. They'd done it! Touchdown pass number 86! After the Colts completed the come-from-behind victory, the two argued over who should keep the ball. Each insisted that the other should have it.

❝ *We're going to try to cut it in half, that's the way it should be.* **❞**

—PEYTON ON WHETHER HE OR HARRISON WOULD KEEP THE BALL FROM THEIR RECORD-BREAKING TOUCHDOWN PASS

The unbeaten Colts weren't just winning—they were crushing every team in their path. But in their eighth game, a familiar foe waited. The Colts traveled to New England to face Brady and the Patriots once again. This time, it was finally Indy's turn to celebrate. Peyton went 28 of 37 for 321 yards and 3 touchdowns in a 40–21 Colts win. With the season half done, Indy still hadn't lost a game. Around the NFL, the buzz about the team's record was picking up. Could the Colts become just the second team in NFL history to go undefeated in the regular season? (At the time, the 1972 Dolphins were the only team ever to do so.)

With each week—and each win—the pressure grew. A 45–37 win over the Cincinnati Bengals pushed Indy's record to 10–0. With wins over the Steelers, Titans, and Jaguars, it grew to 13–0. The Colts had just three games left in the season. Could they win all three? The team had already clinched the AFC South, as well as a first-round bye in the playoffs. Would Dungy rest some of his star players, including Peyton? Getting a game or two off would keep the team rested and healthy for the play-offs. Or would Dungy continue to play his starters in pursuit of a perfect season?

"Those guys want to play, and they want to play all the time," Dungy said. "We don't let them vote, but we will take into consideration how they feel."

In the end, it wasn't a decision Dungy had to make. The Chargers came to the RCA Dome and dealt the Colts a surprising 26–17 loss in the 14th game of the season. The loss was a disappointment for the fans, but some experts thought that it might be a blessing in disguise. The quest for a perfect season was a distraction. Having lost a game, the Colts could get rested and focus on the playoffs. They finished 14–2 after losing one more game.

It had been a magical season for the team and for Peyton, who threw for 3,747 yards and 28 touchdowns. Peyton finished second to Seattle running back Shaun Alexander in the MVP voting. But as always, the team's ultimate success or failure would be determined in the playoffs. After such an impressive regular season, nothing short of a Super Bowl appearance could be considered a success.

After their first-round bye, the Colts hosted the Steelers in the divisional round. The Colts were the AFC's top seed, while the Steelers were the sixth and lowest seed. The Colts had dominated all season, while the Steelers had needed to scratch and claw just to make the playoffs. Indy was heavily favored to advance. But the Steelers rode the momentum of their first-round win and built an early lead. A swarming defense slowed down and confused the powerful Colts attack. As the final minutes of the fourth quarter ticked down, Indianapolis found itself trailing 21–18. Peyton led the team downfield on a final drive. He got the team to the Steelers' 28-yard line, close enough for a field-goal try, but also failed to effectively use all of the time the Colts had. Vanderjagt came onto the field to attempt a game-tying field goal. But the ball sailed wide right. The Steelers had pulled off an amazing upset. The Colts had dominated the league all season, but they'd collapsed once again when it mattered most.

Reporters and fans voiced the same old questions about Peyton's ability to win in the postseason. By the beginning of the next season, he'd be thirty years old. What would his legacy be? Was he destined to go down in history as the greatest NFL quarterback never to reach a Super Bowl?

Chapter Eight

Super Season

As the 2006 season began, lots of experts wondered if the Colts' window of opportunity was closing. The team was getting older. Before the season, James went to the Arizona Cardinals, leaving most of the running back duties to rookie Joseph Addai. Harrison was thirty-four years old—nearly ancient by the standard of most NFL receivers. How many seasons did Peyton and company have before it would be time to rebuild?

Peyton paid little attention to the talk. His focus was the same as it had been every season: winning a Super Bowl. And once again, he led his Colts to a great start. The season opener against the Giants was a big game for the Manning family. Peyton was starting for the Colts, while Eli was starting for the Giants. It was the first time in NFL history that brothers had quarterbacked opposing teams. The media dubbed the game "The Manning Bowl."

"I know [Peyton and Eli] are going to low-key it," Archie said of the boys' approach to playing each other. "They know they're playing a team sport and they've always done that. [Olivia and I are] looking at it that way, too, so we don't want too much attention. We're just going to get through it and hope for a whole lot of offense that night."

Peyton led the Colts to a 16–7 halftime lead. A pass from Eli Manning to Jeremy Shockey in the third quarter cut the lead to 2 points, but the Colts answered back with a touchdown of their own, then held on for a 26–21 win.

The game was the start of another winning streak. In what seemed to be Indy's trademark, the team dominated in the months of September and October. But the streak almost ended in the season's fifth game, against the Titans. The Tennessee defense was shutting down the Colts early, and Indy fell behind 10–0 at halftime. But in the second half, Peyton threw touchdown passes to Harrison and Wayne to edge the Titans 14–13. The game was an example of the Colts' solid defense helping the offense early in the season. However, as the year dragged on, the defense began to falter. Opposing offenses discovered that they could run the ball almost at will against the Colts. It was an ideal strategy, because running the ball and controlling the clock kept the ball out of Peyton's hands.

At first, Peyton and the offense were able to overcome the defense's vulnerability. They were winning high-scoring contests and even managed another victory against the Patriots in New England. Soon, the winning streak had swelled to nine. The Colts had become the first team in NFL history to start out back-to-back seasons 9–0. But the defense's inability to stop the run soon caught up with the team. The Dallas Cowboys beat them in their 10th game, and the Colts would go on to lose three more of their final seven games.

The low point of the season came on December 10 against the Jaguars. The offense started poorly. On their first drive, Peyton saw Harrison streaking down the field, wide open. But he badly underthrew the pass, and Harrison had to slow down to catch it. It went for a 42-yard gain, but a good pass would have been an easy touchdown. The Colts ultimately had to settle for a field goal instead. The Colts' struggles on offense weren't the big story, however. The Jags embarrassed the Colt defense by rushing for 375 yards—the second-highest single-game total since 1970. The embarrassing 44–17 loss was Indy's second in a row. Experts wondered if the Colts were just following a familiar pattern of starting out well only to collapse down the stretch.

The team's late-season stumbles dropped them to 12–4 and cost them a first-round bye in the playoffs. Worse still, few thought the defense could turn things around and provide the support the offense needed.

Indy's Wild Card opponent, the Chiefs, promised to be a good test. They were a team built around a powerful running game—a challenging matchup for the Colts defense. But the defense proved to be up to the task. The Colts kicked 3 field goals in the first half to take a 9–0 halftime lead. In the fourth quarter, Peyton found Wayne in the end zone for a 5-yard, game-sealing touchdown pass. The 23–8 final score was much lower than experts had predicted. But was the success of the Colt defense a fluke, or were they really finally starting to come around?

"Our defense was awesome today," Peyton said. "We made some mistakes and the defense made sure we didn't pay for it."

The next test was against the Baltimore Ravens, a team built around a stifling defense. The game was in Baltimore, where the Ravens had been almost unbeatable during the regular season. It was another defensive battle. In fact, neither team scored a touchdown all game long! In a battle of field goals, Indy's Adam Vinatieri (who had replaced Vanderjagt as the team's kicker) accounted for all 15 Indianapolis points, while the defense held Baltimore to just 6. After such a terrible end to the regular season, it was shocking to see Indy's defense not only playing well but even carrying the offense at times. Suddenly, fans in Indy were optimistic.

The AFC Championship promised to be one of the most intriguing matchups of the year. If the Colts wanted to reach the Super Bowl, they would have to prove themselves against the Patriots. They'd defeated the Patriots during the regular season, but everybody knew that a playoff game was something else entirely for the Colts. The Patriots had won three Super Bowls in recent years. They'd knocked out the Colts on several occasions. The Patriots understandably had a swagger and confidence that the Colts just couldn't match. It was a dream matchup for the NFL, pitting the league's two biggest stars— quarterbacks Peyton and Brady—in a rivalry game for the right to advance to the Super Bowl. But this time, the Colts had one big advantage—the game was held in Indianapolis. Having the home-field advantage can make all the difference, especially in the playoffs, and the Colts hoped to exploit that edge.

The game lived up to the hype. The Patriots scored first on a lucky bounce. Brady fumbled the ball near the goal line, but it rolled toward the end zone, where a New England lineman fell on it for a touchdown. It was a lucky play, but it counted just the same. After a Vinatieri field goal pulled the Colts to within 4 points, the Patriots took control of the game. In the second quarter, running back Corey Dillon capped off a drive with a 7-yard touchdown run. When the Colts got the ball back, Peyton threw an interception that New England returned for a touchdown. Just like that, Indy was trailing 21–3. The RCA Dome crowd was silent. Was history repeating itself? Why couldn't the Colts seem to do anything right against the Patriots?

Peyton remained confident, however. "You don't envision getting down, 21–3, to the New England Patriots," he later said. "It didn't feel like things were going that bad. It was my fault it was 21–3."

After another Vinatieri field goal, the halftime score was 21–6. Peyton and his team had their work cut out for them. Luckily, they would get the ball to start the second half. They slowly, methodically drove the ball down the field. The Patriot defense was preventing deep passes, so Peyton adjusted by calling runs and short passes. He drove the Colts down to the 1-yard line, where he scored the touchdown himself on a quarterback sneak. The punishing drive took 7 minutes off the clock and served as a statement that the Colts weren't going away quietly.

The Colts defense kept the momentum in Indy's favor by forcing a New England punt on the following possession. Trailing by 8 points with a quarter and a half yet to play, the confidence was returning to the Colts' sideline. Once again, Peyton led his offense down to the New England 1-yard line. This time, he took the snap and whipped a quick pass to Dan Klecko, a defensive player who came into the game as a blocker. Touchdown! With the score at 21–19, the Colts decided to try for a 2-point conversion rather than kick the extra point. Peyton dropped back to pass again, and this time found Harrison in the end zone. The game was tied!

> The Colts' comeback from 18 points down in the AFC title game was the biggest comeback in championship-game history.

The teams traded touchdowns, then field goals, so that with a little more than five minutes to play, the score stood at 31–31. New England then took the ball and drove for a field goal and a 3-point lead. Peyton got the ball back at the Indianapolis 20-yard line with just over two minutes in regulation. The Colts needed a field goal to tie the game and force overtime or a touchdown to win it. If the offense failed here, they'd never get the ball back.

Peyton knew that the team had to move quickly. A pass to Wayne got them to midfield. Then Peyton found tight end Bryan Fletcher for a big 32-yard completion. After another completion to Wayne and a New England penalty, the ball was at the 11-yard line. From there, Vinatieri could kick an easy field goal. But the Colts went for the end zone instead. Three plays later, Addai ran the ball for a 3-yard touchdown and a 38–34 lead. One minute remained on the clock. Brady tried to lead the Patriots to a desperate touchdown for the win, but an interception sealed the victory. The Colts had done it! They'd beaten the Patriots and earned a trip to the Super Bowl!

"I'm so proud of the way our guys fought," said Dungy. "I'm very happy for Peyton. He was very, very calm. He had to bring us from behind three or four times. It's just fitting. Our team went the hard way the whole year."

❝ I just wanted to do my job and do my job well. I didn't think I needed to be super. I just needed to be good. ❞

—PEYTON ON HIS PERFORMANCE
AGAINST THE PATRIOTS IN THE AFC TITLE GAME

The media attention leading up to the Super Bowl is always intense, and this time was no exception for Peyton and the Colts. From the moment they arrived in Miami almost a week before game day, reporters were everywhere. Amazingly, questions about Peyton's ability to win the big game were still popping up. Apparently, beating New England in the AFC title game wasn't enough. Peyton would have to win a Super Bowl before they'd go away entirely.

The Colts were heavily favored against the NFC champions, the Chicago Bears. Most experts considered the AFC to be a much stronger conference. Many experts said that if the Bears had been in the AFC, they would have been only the fourth- or fifth-best team in the conference. In many ways, the Bears were the complete opposite of the Colts. They were a team with a punishing, big-play defense but had an offense that struggled to score points. Their quarterback, Rex Grossman, was frequently booed in his own stadium. Most experts felt that if Peyton and the Colts offense could play a conservative game and not have many turnovers (interceptions and fumbles), the Bears wouldn't be able to keep up.

When the long buildup to the game was finally over, Peyton and the Colts were ready. The Bears won the pregame coin toss and elected to receive the opening kickoff. A light rain was falling, and the crowd was deafening as Vinatieri booted the ball to Chicago return man Devin Hester, who caught it near the sideline. Hester ran toward the middle of the field and put on a dizzying series of moves and fakes. Within seconds, he had sped past all of the Colt defenders and was sprinting to the end zone. Just like that, the Bears had erupted to a 7–0 lead. For a team that struggled to score points, Hester's score was a huge boost. For Peyton and his teammates, the touchdown run was one heck of a wake-up call. Things only got worse when Peyton threw an interception on the Colts' opening drive. Peyton was having a hard time throwing precise passes because the ball was wet from the rain. The Bears clamped down on the receivers, too, daring the Colts to run the ball.

The Colts could have panicked, but they didn't. Dungy had prepared his team well. "There will be some storms we might have to weather," he had told his players the night before. This was exactly the sort of storm he was talking about. Dungy remained calm and cool on the sideline, and his team followed his lead.

Peyton and the offense got the ball back. This time, they were ready to even the score. At their own 47-yard line, Peyton dropped back to pass. He spotted Wayne downfield and set himself to launch a deep pass. But a Bear defender slammed into him just as he was releasing the ball. The result was a high, floating pass—the sort of pass that was seriously in danger of being intercepted. But the Colts had some luck on their side. For some reason, Wayne's defender broke the wrong way, and Wayne found himself wide open right under the pass, which went for a 53-yard touchdown. However, the Colts mishandled the snap for the point after and had to settle for just 6 points.

Chicago extended its lead to 14–6 late in the first quarter. But from that point on, the Colts went on to dominate the game. Peyton wasn't as sharp as usual. The wet field and wet ball made a precision passing attack difficult. But the Colts adjusted their game plan and methodically moved the ball down the field. After a Vinatieri field goal and a touchdown from running back Dominic Rhodes, the Colts had a 16–14 halftime lead.

> ❝ *In the past when our team's come up short, it's been disappointing. Somehow, we found a way to have learned from those bad losses, and we've been a better team because of it. As disappointing as the playoff loss was last year to Pittsburgh, the veteran guys got together and learned from it and felt we were a better team this year and maybe stronger for it. It's nice when you put [in] a lot of hard work to cap it off with a championship.* ❞
>
> —PEYTON ON THE COLTS' SUPER BOWL TITLE

In the second half, Grossman and the Bears' offense struggled mightily, while Peyton and the Colts followed the conservative game plan that they knew would succeed. Peyton didn't take any chances, knowing that the Bears' offense would have a tough time coming back. After two third-quarter field goals, they had a 22–14 lead. Then in the fourth quarter, defensive back Kelvin Hayden intercepted a Grossman pass and returned it for a touchdown. When the final second finally ticked off the

clock, the Colts had a 29–17 victory and a Super Bowl championship. The Colts poured onto the field, shaking hands, hug-
ging, giving high fives, and savoring the biggest victory of their
careers. Even though Peyton's numbers weren't great—he completed 25 of 38 passes for 247 yards—he was named the game's
MVP. Nobody could question his big-game ability again.

"[Peyton] did what he did all season," said Colts president
Bill Polian. "He overcomes adversity. Whatever people throw at
him, he handles it."

Peyton didn't want to talk about his legacy after the game.
But Dungy was more than happy to compliment his star quarterback. "If people thought that [Peyton's career wasn't complete without a Super Bowl championship], that's just wrong.
But now, he's done it. He's a Hall of Fame quarterback, one of
the best that's ever played the game."

Indeed. Peyton had enjoyed more than his share of personal honors and records. But nothing could match this one. He
was a Super Bowl champion.

Chapter | Nine

Shining Star

Peyton has long been one of the NFL's brightest stars. He didn't need a Super Bowl title for that. He's well liked, focused on the team, and always concerned about helping others. Many stars don't like to spend too much time signing autographs, but Peyton goes out of his way to make time for the fans. He's an icon in popular culture as well as in sports, starring in countless commercials and appearing on talk shows. He has even hosted the late-night comedy TV show *Saturday Night Live*.

Peyton knows that he's a role model, and he does his best to live up to that. He uses his fame to help people. He's involved with many charities and programs, but one of his favorites is the PeyBack Foundation. Peyton and Ashley started the foundation to give back to the Indianapolis community that has given them so much. One of the foundation's programs is Peyton's Pals. Twenty at-risk children get together with Peyton once a month for activities like pizza parties and sports events. Peyton encourages them to work hard and take advantage of their opportunities in life.

Peyton also enjoys visiting children in Indianapolis-area hospitals. In 2007 St. Vincent Children's Hospital even changed its name to Peyton Manning Children's Hospital at St. Vincent.

Despite all he does off the field, Peyton remains focused on football. Winning a Super Bowl didn't change that. In 2007 he and the Colts came out as sharp as ever, winning their first six games handily. In the team's seventh game, against the Carolina Panthers, Peyton threw his 288th touchdown pass as a Colt, breaking the team record held by Johnny Unitas. The Colts won the game 31–7 to move to 7–0 for the season.

The victory set up one of the most anticipated regular-season matchups the NFL had ever seen. On November 4, the Colts faced off against the undefeated Patriots in Indianapolis. The 8–0 Patriots were enjoying one of the best starts in NFL history. Brady and his receivers, led by Randy Moss, were torching the league. His 30 touchdown passes through 7 games had him on a pace to shatter Peyton's single-season record. Which team would continue its winning streak and take control of the top spot in the AFC?

The two potent offenses started out slowly, with a 21-yard field goal off the foot of Vinatieri scoring the only points of the first quarter. Brady and Moss gave the Patriots a 7–3 lead early in the second quarter. But after another Vinatieri field goal, Peyton found Addai for a 73-yard touchdown pass and a 13–7 halftime lead.

---

66 *[Peyton's] probably got a better arm, he's probably faster, he's bigger, he's probably smarter. He's proven over the years how consistent he is. I've always looked up to Peyton and the way he plays. He's gotten the best of us the last three times we played, so we've got a great challenge. Hopefully we're all up for it.* 99
—Tom Brady on Peyton before their game in 2007

Early in the fourth quarter, following a Patriots field goal, Peyton and the Colts seemed ready to take control of the game. With less than 10 minutes left, Peyton and his offense were on New England's 1-yard line. Peyton ran a quarterback sneak up the middle for the touchdown and a 10-point lead. The RCA Dome crowd went wild. At 20–10, the Colts appeared to have the game firmly in control.

But Brady wasn't done. He took the ball and quickly moved New England down the field, hitting Randy Moss for two long passes before connecting with Wes Welker for a touchdown pass. The Colts got the ball back with eight minutes remaining, but penalties killed the drive and forced them to punt. The Patriots took just three plays to score another touchdown, and when Peyton fumbled on a quarterback sack the next drive, it was over. The Patriots earned the 24–20 comeback win and moved to 9–0 for the season.

BROKEN RECORD

Peyton didn't hold on to the record for passing touchdowns in a season for long. In the Patriots' final game of the season, Tom Brady found Randy Moss for his 50th touchdown pass of the season. On the play, Moss also set the record for receiving touchdowns in a season, with 23. Their great play helped propel New England to a perfect 16–0 regular season.

The loss—and the lack of Marvin Harrison, who was out with an injury—seemed to affect Peyton and the Colts. Peyton played poorly in the team's next game, in San Diego. He threw a career-high six interceptions in a 23–21 loss. A week later, Indy barely escaped embarrassment at home with a 13–10 win over the Chiefs, one of the worst teams in the NFL. Once again, Peyton played poorly, throwing for just 163 yards and no touchdowns. A few weeks earlier, the Colts had seemed almost invincible. But suddenly they looked vulnerable. While the Patriots kept on winning, the Colts were struggling just to hold on to the number-two spot in the conference. Peyton blamed himself and the offense. "We need to start playing a little better offensively and being more efficient and not counting on our defense to hold their offense to 10 points," he said.

Peyton and the Colts soon managed to fix their problems. The win over the Chiefs started a new six-game winning streak that was highlighted by a 28–25 victory over the second-place Jacksonville Jaguars. Peyton's 4 touchdown passes in that game all but clinched the AFC South title for Indy. By the final game of the season, the Colts had secured the number-two seed in the AFC. Because their playoff spot was locked in, many of the team's starters rested in the last game, a 16–10 loss to Tennessee.

Peyton hit more career milestones in 2007. He reached 40,000 passing yards in the victory over the Chiefs. That victory was also the 100th of his career. A few games later, he became only the fifth quarterback in NFL history to throw 300 career touchdown passes.

Having earned a first-round bye, the Colts got another week off to rest and heal. Most experts consider a bye week a big advantage heading into the playoffs. But after the team had rested many of its starters late in the season, some were concerned that all the time off would leave Indy rusty. The test would come January 13 against the Chargers, a team that had beaten the Colts during the regular season. Would Peyton and his offense be ready?

The Chargers were one of the league's hottest teams. They'd started off the 2007 season poorly but had won seven in a row, including their opening-round victory over Tennessee. They had a punishing running game and a tough defense. But despite all of this, many fans and experts fully expected Indianapolis to win. The Colts and Patriots had been the dominant teams in the league all season. A rematch of the previous season's AFC Championship seemed inevitable.

At first, everything seemed to point toward an Indy win. The Colts took the opening kickoff and drove it down the field. Peyton looked sharp, completing several short, crisp passes before hitting tight end Dallas Clark for a 25-yard touchdown. Indy's chances only looked better in the second quarter, when San Diego's star running back, LaDainian Tomlinson, left the game with an injury. (The Chargers' quarterback, Philip Rivers, would also leave the game hurt.) But the Colts couldn't seem to put the undermanned Chargers away. Peyton's mistakes, including a costly interception deep in San Diego territory early in the third quarter, kept the game close. Still, when Peyton found Reggie Wayne for a 9-yard touchdown late in the third quarter, the Colts had a 17–14 lead and appeared to be in control. But San Diego answered back with a touchdown of its own before the end of the quarter.

With just under 11 minutes to play in the game, the Colts trailed 21–17. The Colts defense forced the Chargers to punt. After a short run and an incomplete pass, Indy was facing a third-and-9. Peyton looked at the San Diego defense and snapped the ball. He saw wide receiver Anthony Gonzalez streaking down the left sideline and rifled a pass. Gonzalez pulled it in and darted into the end zone, just barely staying in bounds. The crowd erupted. With the extra point, the Colts had a 24–21 lead.

But once again, the Chargers just wouldn't be outdone. With a second-string running back (Michael Turner) and quarterback (Billy Volek), San Diego took the ball and drove against a tired Colts defense. They moved 78 yards over 8 plays, capped off by a Volek sneak for a touchdown and a 28–24 lead.

Once again, it was Peyton's turn. The Colts took over at their own 23-yard line. Peyton was on fire. On the first play of the drive, he threw to Clark for 14 yards. Then he hit Wayne for

11, Devin Aromashodu for 13, and Gonzalez for 5 yards. After his next two attempts were incomplete, the Colts were facing a fourth-and-5. Peyton calmly found Clark down the middle for 16 yards. A San Diego penalty moved the Colts to the 9-yard line. But after a short run and three incomplete passes, the drive was over.

"We did a good job of moving the ball," Peyton said of the drive. "San Diego tightened up there in the red zone. Of course, it's disappointing that we couldn't get it in there in the end. We got down there, did a good job getting it down there, and just couldn't quite finish it."

Peyton and his offense got the ball one more time with less than 2 minutes remaining, but the San Diego defense held them firmly in place to seal the win. The Chargers had held on for one of the biggest upsets of the season. Shockingly, the Colts' season was over without even a single playoff victory.

After the Colts lost to the Chargers in the playoffs, rumors swirled about Dungy retiring from coaching. But after a week of thinking, Dungy decided to return to the Colts for the 2008 season.

After the game, Peyton was asked if having won a Super Bowl the year before made it easier to accept such a tough loss. "What happened last year doesn't make it any easier this year," he answered. "When you come back and commit yourself to the '07 season and you don't finish it like you want to, it hurts."

Despite the loss, Peyton had a good reason to keep watching the NFL playoffs. Eli and the Giants were playing the heavily favored Dallas Cowboys later that afternoon. Eli had one of the best games of his career, leading the Giants to a 21–17 upset victory. Peyton's season was over, but his little brother still had a shot to reach his first Super Bowl. Eli had often been criticized during the regular season. He had struggled badly at times but had really performed entering the playoffs, helping New York score road wins in Tampa Bay and Dallas. The Giants pulled off yet another upset in the NFC Championship game. In subzero temperatures at Green Bay, the Giants beat the Packers in overtime. Peyton hadn't been able to get back to the Super Bowl, but at least he could root for his brother Eli.

Eli and the Giants took the field against the undefeated Patriots on February 3, 2008. New England was favored to take the game for a perfect season. But Eli and the Giants came out with an opening drive that lasted 10 minutes and ended in a field goal. The drive set the tone for the tough, defensive game. With less than three minutes left, Brady threw a touchdown pass to Randy Moss, putting the Patriots ahead 14–10. Peyton watched from a luxury box as his brother tried to lead New York on a final, game-winning drive.

No Jinxing It

Peyton didn't attend Eli's victory in the NFC Championship game in Green Bay. Earlier in the year, he'd gone to a Giants home game against the Vikings. But Minnesota intercepted Eli four times in an embarrassing 41–17 loss for the Giants. Peyton stayed home so he wouldn't bring his brother more bad luck.

With 1:15 left, Eli and the Giants were facing third-and-5 from their own 44. Eli snapped the ball and dropped back. The Patriot defense was in hot pursuit, grabbing and almost sacking him. But Eli broke free and heaved a pass downfield. Receiver David Tyree leaped and made an amazing 32-yard catch to keep the Giants' hopes alive. A few plays later, Eli found receiver Plaxico Burress wide open in the end zone for the touchdown, taking the lead. The Giants' defense sealed the deal, keeping the Patriots from scoring on their final possession. Peyton pumped his fist as the final seconds ticked away. A year after Peyton had won his first Super Bowl ring, his brother had done the same. And like Peyton, Eli was named the Super Bowl MVP.

"This has been Eli's year," Peyton said after the game. "I am proud to have been here tonight. I am proud to be his brother and I love him very much."

Epilogue

Peyton's Legacy

U nitas, Bradshaw, Marino, Montana, Elway. They're just a few of the names that come up when discussing the greatest quarterback in NFL history. Does Peyton's name belong alongside theirs on that list? It's always hard to judge a player's place in history until he's retired. And it's almost impossible to compare quarterbacks of different eras—the passing game of the modern NFL scarcely resembles the way Unitas played.

Despite all of that, Manning's place on the list seems all but assured. He's already shattered many NFL passing records and is on pace to set quite a few more. With his Super Bowl win in 2007, he took the leap from great quarterback to great championship quarterback.

The numbers he has amassed are staggering. His 306 career touchdown passes already rank fourth on the all-time list, while his 41,626 passing yards rank him ninth. He's fourth in completion percentage and second in passer rating. Meanwhile, his average of more than 260 passing yards per game is the highest in league history. And his durability is almost as impressive as his raw talent. He hasn't missed a game in his NFL career, a streak of 160 games over his first 10 seasons.

Even if Peyton never played another game, he'd be a lock for football's Hall of Fame. But retirement won't be coming anytime soon. How long can Peyton keep putting up such astonishing numbers? After the 2007 season, he was still just thirty-one years old. Many quarterbacks continue to be effective into their forties. If that's the case for Peyton, almost no record seems out of reach. He may well go down as the greatest quarterback the league has ever seen.

PERSONAL STATISTICS

Name:

Peyton Williams Manning

Born:

March 24, 1976, New Orleans, Louisiana

College:

University of Tennessee

Height:

6'5"

Weight:

230 lbs.

Throws:

Right-handed

COLLEGE STATISTICS

Year	Team	Games	Att	Comp	Yards	TD	Int
1994	Tenn.	10	144	89	1,141	11	6
1995	Tenn.	11	380	244	2,954	22	4
1996	Tenn.	11	380	243	3,287	20	12
1997	Tenn.	12	477	287	3,819	36	11
Career		44	1,381	863	11,201	89	33

Key: Att: attempts; Comp: completions; TD: touchdowns; Int: interceptions

PROFESSIONAL STATISTICS

Year	Team	Games	Att	Comp	Yards	TD	Int
1998	IND	16	575	326	3,739	26	28
1999	IND	16	533	331	4,135	26	15
2000	IND	16	571	357	4,413	33	15
2001	IND	16	547	343	4,131	26	23
2002	IND	16	591	392	4,200	27	19
2003	IND	16	566	379	4,267	29	10
2004	IND	16	497	336	4,557	49	10
2005	IND	16	453	305	3,747	28	10
2006	IND	16	557	362	4,397	31	9
2007	IND	16	515	337	4,040	31	14
Career		160	5,405	3,468	41,626	306	153

Key: Att: attempts; Comp: completions; TD: touchdowns; Int: interceptions

GLOSSARY

blitz: a defensive play in which defenders who don't usually rush the quarterback do so

Bowl Alliance: a short-lived agreement between college football conferences in an effort to provide quality bowl games. The Bowl Alliance lasted from 1995 to 1997.

draft: a system for selecting new players for professional sports teams

endorse: to promote a product in advertisements

incentive: a part of a contract that calls for additional money to be paid for certain achievements

pocket: the protected area behind a team's offensive line, in which the quarterback usually operates

rookie: a first-year player

scholarship: money given to a student to help pay the costs of schooling

Wild Card: a team that earns a playoff spot despite not winning its division. The NFL awards Wild Card spots to the top two nondivision winners in each conference.

BIBLIOGRAPHY

BOOKS

Hyams, Jimmy. *Peyton Manning: Primed and Ready*. Lenexa, KS:
    Addax Publishing Group, 1998.

Manning, Archie and Peyton. *Manning*. New York:
    HarperEntertainment, 2000.

SELECTED ARTICLES

Battista, Judy. "Colts Overcome Brady and Patriots to Reach
    Super Bowl." *New York Times*. January 22, 2007.
    http://www.nytimes.com/2007/01/22/sports/
    football/22afc.html (February 20, 2008).

CNN/SI. "Like Father, Like Son." *Sportsillustrated.com*. April 20,
    1998. http://sportsillustrated.cnn.com/football/nfl/
    events/1998/nfldraft/news/1998/04/20/manning
    _package/ (February 20, 2008).

Hack, Damon. "FOOTBALL: Manning and Dungy a Not-So-Odd
    Couple." *New York Times*. July 25, 2002. http://query
    .nytimes.com/gst/fullpage.html?res=9D04E6D91038F936
    A15754C0A9649C8B63 (February 20, 2008).

WEB SITES

Colts.com

http://www.colts.com

The official home page of the Indianapolis Colts includes all the latest team news and statistics with photos, videos, and more.

ESPN.com—Peyton Manning

http://sports.espn.go.com/nfl/players/profile?statsId=4256

ESPN.com's player page on Peyton includes career statistics, feature articles, and a game log.

NFL.com—The Official Site of the National Football League

http://www.nfl.com

The NFL's official site includes scores, news, statistics, video features, and other information for football fans.

PeytonManning.com

http://peytonmanning.com

Peyton's official site is packed with news from on and off the field with a team schedule, photos, statistics, and information on the PeyBack Foundation.

INDEX

103